With heart & hope ~

[signature]

The Little Girl Who Found IT

A Story of Heart and Hope

the little IT series

Janae Bower

illustrated by John Bower, Sr.

Andover, MN

ISBN 1-931945-05-5

Library of Congress Catalog Number: 2003104223

Printed in Korea

First Printing: July 2003

07 06 05 04 03   6 5 4 3 2 1

Expert Publishing, Inc.
14314 Thrush Street NW, Andover, MN 55304-3330
1-877-755-4966
www.expertpublishinginc.com

To order, visit *www.innerconnections.biz.*
Quantity discounts available.

Dedication

Dedicated to my husband, John,
for inspiring me to wholeheartedly
live my dreams.

Keepsake Page

To: _____

From: _____

Receiving it warms the heart.

Reading it inspires hope.

Dear Reader

Dear girls,

May your heart be full of hope
and may you hope with all your
heart.

—Janae Bower

There once was a little girl just as happy as can be

2

Her life was filled with joy and love when she was young and free.

Being so young
Playing a ton

Loving everyone.

Never in a hurry
Never with a
worry

6

Living **IT** was fun.

But suddenly
something
changed.

8

The little girl grew up.

What she did as a little girl
Evolved into a spinning whirl.

Being young was not like
the same as before
She longed to be mature,
not young anymore.

11

Having fun was not playing with toys
Fun was when girls were kissing the boys.

Loving everyone was not
the way to be
Being "in" by leaving
people out was key.

Never in a hurry, what did it all once mean?
There were so many things to do as a teen.

Never with a worry, that's not here
Having IT meant better things were near.

Everything she did, she did so she'd fit in
Otherwise she would never find IT again.

She was as happy as could be
Living how she thought IT should be.

But suddenly
something
changed.

18

The little girl grew up more.

19

Everything she did as a teen
Now she wondered, what did it mean?

She left home hoping to find
IT out there
She didn't know what and
didn't know where.

She studied and learned as much as she could
If this didn't help her find IT , what would?

Getting a job or career
She was sure she'd find IT here.

Working 9 to 5 was fun at first
Until the magical bubble burst.

If only she became a wife
This would bring IT to her life.

So she searched and
searched a ton
Until she found the right one.

She married and started her life as two
She didn't find ∏ , now what would she do?

If she had children—that she knew
IT would come, so her family grew.

She was as happy as could be
Living how she thought ∏ should be.

But suddenly
something
changed.

30

The little **girl grew old.**

With everything she had done until now
She couldn't find π and didn't know how.

When it was time to
say goodbye
She still hadn't found
IT and wondered why.

She looked out the window feeling so sad
And saw her granddaughter happy and glad.

And suddenly she changed!

36

The little girl grew wise.

This is what she
needed to say
With what she's
learned along the way,

"All my life I've been looking for IT, now it's plain to see
To live a life of heart and hope, IT has to start with me!"

IT can't come from others, IT comes from within
A special part of you that has always been.

When you believe
in yourself and
the One above
Your life will be
full of meaning,
joy, peace, and
love.

Your heart will shine; hope will grow.
IT 's a journey—long and slow.

My journey started young and free
It was inside, a part of me.

I grew up and as a teen I hid
Being like my friends—that's
what I did.

44

I grew up more with more to learn
I thought IT was something to earn.

Then when I grew old with nothing left to explore,
I found I͡T's a blessing within I can adore.

When IT comes from the heart of you,
Then there is hope in all you do.

She was as happy as happy as can be
Finally living life the way IT ought to be!

The End

Special Acknowledgements

My heartfelt thanks and appreciation to:

John Bower Sr., my father-in-law and talented artist, for the gift of your illustrations. You magically captured the essence of the story!

Ken and Sheila Opatz, my parents, for the gift of roots to grow and wings to fly.

Family and friends, for the gift of precious support and feedback with the book.

Janet Hagberg, my spiritual teacher, for the gift of grace and wisdom.

Harry and Sharron Stockhausen, my publishers, for the gift of bringing this book to life.

Author

Janae Bower is an inspirational teacher and business consultant. She founded InnerConnections, a training and consulting company that works with organizations and individuals to create inspired workplaces with measurable results. With expertise in human resource development and spirit in the workplace, she inspires others to wholeheartedly live their dreams! Janae lives in Minnesota with her husband, John.

Order Information

Give the gift of The Little Girl Who Found IT: A Story of Heart and Hope to your family and friends.

Email janae@innerconnections.biz or go to www.innerconnections.biz for:

- ordering information
- quantity discounts
- fundraising options
- presentations and workshops